THE STORY OF
NIKE

A A R O N   F R I S C H

A⁺

Published by Smart Apple Media
1980 Lookout Drive, North Mankato, Minnesota 56003

Copyright © 2004 Smart Apple Media.
International copyrights reserved in all countries.
No part of this book may be reproduced in any form without
written permission from the publisher.

Photographs by AP/Wide World (Emile Wamsteker), Corbis (Vernier Jean Bernard,
Bohemian Nomad Picturemakers, Duomo, Sandy Felsenthal, James Leynse,
Mark Peterson, Steve Raymer), Getty Images/Time Life (Urbano Delvalle,
Andrew Holbrooke, James Keyser, Alan Levenson, Robin Moyer, Co Rentmeester,
Dale Wittner), Icon Sports Media (Action Images, Action Plus, John Cordes,
Icon Sports Photos, John McDonough, Philippe Millereau/DPPI, STL),
Unicorn Stock Photos (Aneal Vohra)

Library of Congress Cataloging-in-Publication Data
Frisch, Aaron.
The story of Nike / by Aaron Frisch.
p. cm. — (Built for success)
Summary: Describes the founding and development of the Nike
company, makers of athletic shoes with the famous "swoosh" logo.
Includes bibliographical references.
ISBN 1-58340-295-0
1. Nike (Firm)—History—Juvenile literature. 2. Sporting goods
industry—United States—History—Juvenile literature. 3. Footwear
industry—United States—History—Juvenile literature. 4. Athletic
shoes—History—Juvenile literature. [1. Nike (Firm).] I. Title. II. Series.
HD9992.U54 N5535 2003
338.7'6887'0973—dc21
2002036566

688.76

24689753

THE STORY OF

NIKE

Table of Contents

A Blue-Ribbon Beginning **4**

A Company with "Sole" **13**

Just Do It **23**

Success . . . and Setbacks **30**

A Global Leader **36**

Important Moments Time Line **42**

Glossary **44**

Index **46**

Further Information **48**

A Blue-Ribbon Beginning

Nike has taken the sneaker and turned it into an international empire. In 2002, the company sold more than $9.9 billion in athletic shoes, apparel, and equipment. It also continued to place its products on the world's greatest athletes. How did it all begin?

Back in the early 1960s, a young Oregon graduate student and middle-distance runner named Philip Knight wanted to write a term paper about something he enjoyed. He thought of an interesting topic: how to design and sell track shoes. After researching the industry, Knight believed he could start his own company by buying low-cost shoes in Japan and selling them in the United States.

On Thanksgiving Day in 1962, Knight boarded a plane for Japan. There, he visited a sporting goods store and saw a pair of running shoes with the brand name "Tiger," manufactured by a company called Onitsuka. Knight took a train to the city of Kobe to meet with executives of the company. He told Onitsuka that he was a shoe **importer** from the U.S. When asked the name of his company, Knight had to think fast. He

said the first thing that popped into his head, calling his new company "Blue Ribbon Sports."

Knight's first order, five pairs of white and blue leather Tiger shoes, did not arrive in the U.S. until more than a year after his trip to Japan. Knight and Bill Bowerman, his former track coach at the University of Oregon, each chipped in $500 to import more shoes. Bowerman agreed to **promote** the shoes to college athletes. Knight would handle everything else. Less than one year later, Knight had sold 1,300 pairs of running shoes out of the trunk of his car and from card tables

Phil Knight founded the Nike empire four decades ago

set up at local track meets. He supported his fledgling business by working as an accountant.

In the early 1960s, American companies sold a lot of sneakers—comfortable and inexpensive shoes that people wore for leisure. German manufacturers such as Adidas, however, were known to make the best athletic shoes. Most serious track-and-field athletes wore Adidas, but Knight thought he could compete against the German company. He believed he could sell his shoes for less than Adidas shoes and still make a nice profit.

In 1965, Knight met Jeff Johnson—one of his former running rivals—at a track meet. Knight approached him about

Phil Knight

Philip Hampson Knight grew up in a suburb of Portland, Oregon. Known to his childhood friends as "Buck," he enjoyed athletics but wasn't big enough or tall enough to excel at football or basketball. As a teen, he took up track and field instead.

During his high school years, Knight took a summer job on the night shift at a newspaper. When he finished his shift, he would jog the seven miles (11 km) from work to home. When he enrolled at the University of Oregon, Knight joined the track team, coached by a fiery and passionate running enthusiast named Bill Bowerman. The coach would later help Knight start the Blue Ribbon Sports company.

Knight has lived in the same house, set on five acres (2 ha) of land in Oregon, since the mid-1970s. He lives there with his wife Penny, whom he met when they were students at Portland State in Oregon. Today, Knight's stake in Nike makes him one of the wealthiest men in the U.S., with an estimated net worth of more than $5 billion.

Bill Bowerman made Oregon America's running capital

promoting Tiger shoes, and Johnson agreed to sell them on a part-time basis. Knight offered Johnson an advance of $400 and an income based on **commission**. By the end of that year, Blue Ribbon Sports had sold $20,000 worth of Tiger shoes and made a profit of about $3,200.

In 1966, Johnson sold so many shoes that Knight hired him as the company's first full-time employee. Johnson started handing out T-shirts with the Tiger name across the front to promote their products. Soon the T-shirts were so popular that Johnson and Knight decided to sell them as well.

Over the years, Phil Knight has remained a hands-on leader

They opened their first retail store on Pico Boulevard in Santa Monica, California.

Although jogging is now one of the most popular forms of exercise in the world, not many people in the 1960s were interested in it. Bill Bowerman was passionate about it. He explained to his students that jogging could improve a person's heart and lungs, burn body fat, and build endurance. Best of all, anyone could do it. It required no equipment—just a good pair of shoes. In 1967, Bowerman co-authored the book *Jogging: A Physical Fitness Program for All Ages*. It sold more than one mil-

Nike played a major role in the jogging boom of the 1970s

lion copies and earned Bowerman a reputation as an expert on running and running shoes.

During that time, Bowerman designed a shoe that combined the best features of several other shoes. He showed it to executives at Onitsuka, who liked his design and manufactured the shoe just in time for the 1968 Olympics in Mexico City. Blue Ribbon named the shoe the Cortez, and it became one of the best-selling shoes that Bowerman and Knight would market as partners.

Bowerman next suggested to Onitsuka that it make a track shoe from nylon. Onitsuka elaborated on his idea, making a rubber-soled marathon shoe with a thin layer of foam sandwiched between two sheets of nylon. The shoe was lighter than anything made of leather or heavier fabrics such as canvas. The Tiger Marathon, as it was called, changed the athletic shoe market forever.

Blue Ribbon Sports secured an **exclusive contract** to sell the Tiger Marathon, and the company earned nearly $83,000 in shoe sales in 1967. In 1969, sales reached $400,000. One year later, the company earned $1 million, but

Steve Prefontaine (right) was one of Nike's first celebrity spokespeople

it also found itself in trouble. Sales were good, but Blue Ribbon's operating costs had soared as well. In addition, Onitsuka sometimes had difficulty shipping the larger orders on time, and customers did not like the delays.

Facing these complications, Knight and Bowerman decided to create their own brand. They designed a new shoe, but they still needed cash to manufacture their products. To generate the necessary funds, they decided to sell part of the company. By the fall of 1971, **investors** owned about 35 percent of Blue Ribbon Sports. Buoyed by the added funds, Knight and Bowerman were soon promoting a new line of shoes, which they called Nike.

The Swoosh is the most recognized athletic logo on Earth

A Company with "Sole"

In June 1971, Blue Ribbon's first shoes with the new Nike "Swoosh" logo went on sale. Unfortunately, there was a major glitch. The shoes were made in the warm climate of Mexico, and no one had tested them in cold weather. The soles cracked, and the shoes had to be sold at a reduced price. The company had manufactured 10,000 pairs, and almost all were sold for just $7.95.

In October of that year, Knight flew to Japan with a new **line of credit** from a powerful Japanese trading company called Nissho Iwai. With this credit, Knight ordered 6,000 pairs of the popular Tiger Cortez, but now he requested that Onitsuka put Nike's logo on every pair. On the same trip to Japan, he purchased basketball and wrestling shoes, as well as casual street shoes, from other Japanese manufacturers.

In 1972, the U.S. Men's Track and Field Olympic Trials were held in Eugene, Oregon. Athletes from all over the country came to compete for a chance to make the Olympic team. It was at this event that a young runner from the University of Oregon named Steve Prefontaine (who was trained by Bill

Nike's Swoosh is at home in all sports, in all parts of the world

Bowerman) became famous. Blue Ribbon's growing influence was obvious at the trials, as the company's shoes could be seen on the feet of Prefontaine and many other top athletes.

That year, Bowerman had a shoe design epiphany. One day, he poured some liquid **latex** into his wife's hot waffle iron. The result was a ruined waffle iron and a solid piece of latex with a square pattern. Bowerman believed it would make an excellent shoe sole. He brought the sample to Knight, who liked the idea of a textured, latex sole that would give runners and football players better **traction**.

At a 1972 sporting goods show, Nike introduced improved versions of its old shoes, as well as a series of new models featuring a special heel that relieved pressure on the back of the foot. The company also introduced its first shoes designed especially for women. By the end of the year, Blue Ribbon Sports recorded a 60 percent increase in sales, selling 250,000 pairs of running shoes and 50,000 pairs of basketball shoes.

Business was booming, but Blue Ribbon Sports had a problem. It had a contract with Onitsuka to sell only Tiger shoes in the U.S. When Onitsuka learned that its only

American partner was selling other Japanese-made shoes, it decided to find other **distributors**. Knight filed a lawsuit against Onitsuka in 1973, charging that Onitsuka had broken its contract. Onitsuka countered by charging that Blue Ribbon had used the Tiger **trademark** illegally to push the sales of Nike shoes. At the end of this bitter dispute, a judge allowed both Blue Ribbon Sports and Onitsuka to sell the shoe designs they had worked on together. Only Blue Ribbon, how-ever, could use the model names, such as Cortez.

Swoosh—The Nike Logo

In 1970, Phil Knight and his partners needed a logo, a symbol that people would associate with the company. They wanted something that suggested movement and speed and would set them apart from other shoe companies. Adidas, for example, had stripes on the arch of its shoes. Puma had a stripe that ran along the sides of its shoes.

Knight asked Carolyn Davidson, an art student he knew, to come up with several logo designs. After reviewing her sketches, Knight and his partners finally settled on a logo that looked like a rounded check mark. Over time, the new logo became known as the "Swoosh." For her work, Davidson charged Knight $35.

Knight knew he also needed a name to print on the shoe boxes. He and his partners considered such names as Falcon, Bengal, and Dimension 6. None of them really fit the image the company wanted to project. Salesman Jeff Johnson suggested Nike, the name of the winged goddess of victory in Greek mythology. It fit perfectly with the logo because the Swoosh design looked a little like a wing.

Blue Ribbon Sports officially changed its name to Nike in 1978. But the logo has become so well-known that many of Nike's products no longer carry the name—just the famous Swoosh.

Above, running shoes with the Nike Air cushioning system;
left, 1980s basketball shoes; right, shoe manufacturing in China

By 1975, a large number of Americans had become interested in fitness and jogging. People who had never exercised in their lives now wanted to jog in a pair of light, comfortable athletic shoes. But it wasn't only health-conscious runners who wanted Blue Ribbon's shoes. The company earned a total of $8 million in 1975, and $2 million of that was earned selling shoes for basketball, a sport that was becoming increasingly popular with American teenagers.

Over the next few years, Blue Ribbon Sports made great strides in shoe design. A former NASA engineer named Frank Rudy came up with an idea to reduce the shock that feet absorbed when running and jumping on hard pavement. He suggested placing pockets of air inside the shoe's sole to cushion the foot. Knight liked the idea, but the first shoes did not hold up well—the air pockets deflated after a hard jog. Knight encouraged Rudy to keep working on the project and hired him to work for Blue Ribbon Sports.

Knight and his team introduced a shoe called the Tailwind in 1979, just after the company name was changed to Nike. The Tailwind was very light, and the sole had tiny bags

filled with gas—a cushioning system that came to be called Nike Air. Athletes could run, jump, and play as hard as they wanted, and their shoes would spring back to their original shape. This allowed athletes to train harder and longer and reduced the risk of injury.

In 1980, Nike pulled in $269 million, replacing Adidas as the most popular athletic shoe in the U.S. Nike also created a clothing line that included running shorts and T-shirts. Athletic apparel became a major area of growth for the company over the next several years. By 1982, the company's

Nike's line of apparel includes lightweight clothing and caps

clothing line included nearly 200 different products and generated $70 million in sales.

Growing rapidly, Nike began to sell **stock** to the public. In Blue Ribbon's early years, friends and family members had pitched in $5,000 each when Knight needed money to keep the company going. By the early 1980s, their investments in Nike had skyrocketed to a value of $3 million each. Some estimates suggested that those shares were worth about $30 million by the year 2000.

Nike is headquartered in a sprawling, scenic campus in Oregon

Just Do It

Knight learned early on that **endorsements** were a great way to spread the word about Nike. He believed that if he could associate his product with sports heroes, it would give Nike a huge boost. As early as 1973, Knight pursued famous athletes to endorse his line of shoes.

Track star Steve Prefontaine became Nike's first spokesperson when Knight and Bowerman agreed to pay for his training if he wore their shoes. Prefontaine was known as a fiery runner who never settled for anything less than being the best. He won several national collegiate championships, and in June 1970, he appeared on the cover of *Sports Illustrated*. Sadly, Prefontaine's promising career was cut short when he died in a car accident in 1975. At the time of his death, he held seven U.S. track records.

By the summer of 1975, Knight had signed several top National Basketball Association (NBA) players, including Elvin Hayes, Spencer Haywood, and Rudy Tomjanovich. Each player received $2,000 a year and a small **royalty** from profits on Nike basketball shoes. The cost of convincing such big-name

No athlete has done more to boost Nike than Michael Jordan

players to endorse a product rose quickly as athletes recognized their value. By the late 1970s, companies were paying NBA players up to $10,000 to wear their shoes.

At the 1980 Olympic Trials, athletes who wore Nike shoes dominated many events. College baseball and football players and coaches were on the Nike payroll. The company also signed a young tennis player named John McEnroe for $25,000. McEnroe was the top tennis money-maker of the day, and he earned a lot of media attention with his fiery personality and frequent on-court temper tantrums.

Air Jordan

In June 1984, Michael Jordan left college to join the Chicago Bulls in the National Basketball Association. Jordan was an instant superstar, doing things on the court that seemed impossible. Off the court, he was a friendly and magnetic celebrity very much at ease in the spotlight.

Nike executives wanted Jordan to wear their shoes, but he had other offers from Converse and Adidas. In the end, Nike offered him a more attractive package than the other companies: a reported $2.5 million over five years, his own line of Nike basketball shoes, called Air Jordan, and a royalty for each pair of Air Jordan shoes sold. In exchange, he agreed to wear only Nike shoes during games and to help promote the company and its products.

In April 1985, the first Air Jordans hit the stores. They were an instant sensation. Television commercials that showed Jordan soaring through the air for a slam dunk had children, teenagers, and adults lining up to buy the shoes. In Nike's Los Angeles store, the first two shipments of Air Jordans sold out in three days. Another store requested 100,000 pairs of Air Jordans to meet demand. In the first year, customers bought $130 million worth of Air Jordan shoes.

Nike and its athletes did not promote the shoes themselves as much as they promoted the athletic ideals of sacrifice, hard work, and achievement. The company's list of endorsers soon included tennis player Andre Agassi, soccer star Ronaldo, and Dallas Cowboys quarterback Troy Aikman. Nike also signed top women athletes, such as tennis player Monica Seles and runner Joan Benoit-Samuelson.

In 1984, Nike signed Michael Jordan, the Chicago Bulls star now generally regarded as the best basketball player of all time. More than a decade later, Nike set its sights

Brazilian soccer star Ronaldo promoted Nike in South America

Marion Jones is the world's fastest woman and a Nike endorser

on one of the most popular sports figures of the day: Tiger Woods. In August 1996, Knight paid about $40 million to secure the endorsement of the 20-year-old golfer, who had just won his third consecutive national amateur championship.

Nike built new product lines and marketing campaigns around these athletes, forging an attitude that was distinctly Nike: hardworking, competitive, and tough. Nike often featured less-famous athletes, and even ordinary people, with the "Just Do It" slogan to emphasize that anyone can be an athlete—all it takes is sweat and dedication. In the mid-1990s, Nike introduced advertisements aimed at female athletes. The "Girls in the Game" **ad campaign** showed women participating—and excelling—in a variety of sports. One Nike T-shirt bore the slogan, "I am woman. Watch me score."

In the late 1990s and early 21st century, Nike put its shoes and equipment on the bodies of such elite athletes as track-and-field star Marion Jones, cyclist Lance Armstrong, and New York Yankees shortstop Derek Jeter. Other athletic equipment companies also sign famous sports figures, but Nike has long paid big money for the brightest stars.

Endorsements increase the profiles of both Nike and its athletes

Success...and Setbacks

From 1980 through 2002, in every year except 1987, Nike shoes were the top-selling athletic footwear in the world. In 1987, Nike executives failed to recognize the newest trend in fitness, a type of exercise called aerobics. The company fell into second place behind Reebok, whose aerobic shoes sold well. That misstep aside, Nike enjoyed increased sales every year through 1998.

In 1991, Nike became the only sports and fitness company ever to earn more than $3 billion. Then, from 1995 to 1997, the company grew at an astounding rate. In 1995, Nike's revenues totaled about $3 billion. By the end of 1997, the company had sold more than $9 billion of shoes, clothing, and equipment. Along the way, it came to be regarded as "cool" streetwear by customers in their teens and 20s, and Nike clothing sales soared.

But in 1998, Nike seemed to hit a wall as its overall sales dropped off by eight percent. Sales in the Asian market, a region that couldn't get enough of Nike products in the past, fell sharply. The company sold 50 percent of the athletic shoes

in the world in 1998, but that was a lower percentage than the company had enjoyed the year before.

Knight thought that Nike had gotten too big too fast and had become less efficient. To fix this, he decided he would have to **lay off** 1,600 Nike employees and reduce the company's annual operating costs by almost $200 million. However, he was not about to give up the expensive, big-name endorsements that helped Nike become a worldwide winner. Nike spent nearly $1 billion marketing its products in 1998, the same amount it had spent the year before.

Nike has today tapped into almost all parts of the global market

Above and left, Nike employees making shoes in Asian factories;
right, demonstrations against Nike's employment practices

Nike had another problem. Critics began to accuse the company of mistreating its overseas employees. News reports said that the company allowed its Asian factories to pay their workers unfair wages. Overseas managers often hired under-age employees as young as 14 years old, and workers claimed that supervisors would not let them leave work until they met a daily **quota**. Many Nike factories also used dangerous chemicals in the manufacturing process without installing proper equipment to ensure the safety of their employees.

Faced with these charges, Knight in 1998 pledged to stop the mistreatment of Nike employees at overseas factories. He promised that the company would establish a minimum hiring age in its factories, and that Nike would tighten air-quality standards at the sites so that employees would not work for hours on end in a toxic environment. "We believe that these are practices which conscientious, good companies will follow in the 21st century," Knight said.

In the first few years of the 21st century, Nike's earnings slowly rebounded from the setback in 1998. By 2002, the company's revenues had inched up to $9.9 billion. During these years, most of the company's growth occurred outside the U.S. Knight had long dreamed of turning Nike into a truly global corporation, and rising sales in Europe, Asia, and South America were proof of the company's ever-growing reach.

Nike's increased foreign sales were due largely to innovations in soccer footwear and apparel. Soccer is the most popular sport worldwide, and Nike gained a valuable hold in this market in the late 1990s by introducing a soccer shoe called the Mercurial. Many teams from around the world wore Nike shoes in the 2002 World Cup, hosted by South Korea and Japan. During the event, fans bought 150,000 soccer jerseys made by Nike.

Nike's broadening influence was evident in the 2002 World Cup

A Global Leader

Nike headquarters in Beaverton, Oregon, are a symbol of the company's success and unique vision. The 74-acre (30 ha) facility is surrounded by woods and has running paths, lakes, and a high-tech fitness center. Buildings on the sprawling campus are named after famous athletes such as John McEnroe, Michael Jordan, and Lance Armstrong. Nike employees can work out at the Bo Jackson Fitness Center, named after the first athlete to play two professional sports at the same time (baseball for the Kansas City Royals and football for the Los Angeles Raiders), and the company gives a bonus to those who bike to work rather than drive.

Nike has made shopping a unique experience, too, by opening superstores called Nike Towns. These stores sell an amazing array of products, including virtually every current model of Nike athletic shoes, and feature basketball courts and giant statues of sports heroes. The first Nike Town opened in Portland, Oregon, in November 1990. Today there are Nike Towns in cities around the world. When the Tokyo Nike Town opened in Japan, it sold $1 million worth of merchandise in just three days. The Chicago Nike Town is one of the city's top tourist attractions.

When Nike's U.S. sales leveled out in the late '90s, the company began to tap into new corners of the sports market. In 1998, it unveiled a new line of golf shoes and apparel endorsed by Tiger Woods. Nike's global golf sales promptly rose 81 percent. The company also initiated a bigger ad campaign to market its growing line of women's footwear and apparel, and expanded its All Conditions Gear (ACG) line of products designed for outdoor pursuits such as hiking, kayaking, and biking.

Nike continued its tradition of **innovation** in sports technology with a groundbreaking line of body suits unveiled

Nike in Foreign Markets

Sales of footwear and apparel to customers in foreign regions are becoming a bigger and bigger part of Nike's business. The statistics below show the global distribution of Nike's earnings during the 2002 **fiscal year**.

Total revenue:	$9.9 billion
United States:	$4.9 billion
Europe:	$2.7 billion
Asia:	$1.2 billion
Americas (not including the U.S.):	$568 million
Other:	$466 million

Source: 2002 Nike Annual Report

Cathy Freeman wore a Nike Swift Suit in the 2000 Olympic Games

in 2000. The form-fitting suits—which were given such names as the Swift Suit, Swift Spin, and Swift Skin—were the result of years of research and testing in wind tunnels. By carefully combining an array of lightweight, elastic fibers, Nike's design team created a "second skin" that made athletes' bodies more **aerodynamic**. Different suits were made specifically for sprinters, speedskaters, swimmers, cyclists, and other athletes whose goal is to go as fast as possible.

Nike's position as the global leader in athletic apparel was solidified as many of the world's top athletes rose to new

Nike has become a major player in Hong Kong's athletic market

levels of greatness in the 2000 and 2002 Olympics wearing the Swoosh logo. Australian runner Cathy Freeman, track-and-field star Marion Jones, speedskater Apollo Anton Ohno, and others captured gold medals and set new world records wearing the new Nike Swift body suits.

Nike is always coming up with new, innovative products—and equally innovative ways to sell them. "First and foremost, we are a company dedicated to innovation and the passion to create great product," Phil Knight noted in 2001. "From Bowerman's Waffle Trainer to the Tour Accuracy golf ball, we make every effort to take consumers where they want to go before they realize they want to go there."

As the company sets its goals for the 21st century, Phil Knight and his team will continue to come up with creative ideas to sell Nike shoes and athletic products to the world. There are other sports apparel companies that would like to knock Nike from its perch, but Knight is prepared for the fight. He believes his company will remain the world's undisputed champion in athletic shoes and products well into the future.

Tiger Woods is on track to go down as history's greatest golfer

1957   Phil Knight meets Bill Bowerman, a track-and-field coach at the University of Oregon.

1962   Knight and Bowerman start a running shoe company called Blue Ribbon Sports.

1964   Blue Ribbon Sports sells 1,300 pairs of shoes and earns $8,000.

1966   Blue Ribbon Sports opens its first retail store.

1970   Carolyn Davidson designs the now-famous Swoosh logo.

1971   The Nike brand is launched at the U.S. Olympic trials.

1972   American runner Steve Prefontaine becomes the first major track star to wear Nike shoes.

1973   Nike's Waffle Trainer becomes the best-selling training shoe in the U.S.

1980   Nike replaces Adidas as the top-selling brand of athletic shoes in the U.S.

1986   Nike's earnings reach $1 billion.

1988   The "Just Do It" ad campaign sparks new consumer interest in Nike products.

1990   Nike World, the company's corporate headquarters, opens in Beaverton, Oregon.

1991   Nike becomes the first sports company to earn more than $3 billion.

1992 The company's second Nike Town, located in downtown Chicago, opens.

1996 Critics accuse Nike of mistreating employees in its overseas factories.

1999 With sales slumping, Nike lays off seven percent of its workforce, or 1,600 employees.

2002 Nike's annual earnings reach an all-time high of $9.9 billion.

Nike designs footwear for nearly every sport and activity

GLOSSARY

ad campaign A series of advertisements with a common theme.

aerodynamic Able to move through air or water with very little resistance.

commission Money paid to salespeople by their employer as a percentage of their sales.

distributors Individuals or companies that sell and deliver another company's product to retail stores.

endorsements Business deals in which a well-known person is paid to express approval of a product.

exclusive contract An agreement between two parties in which they promise to do business only with each other in a given market.

fiscal year A 12-month schedule by which a company keeps records of its earnings; it differs by company and usually does not correspond to the calendar year.

importer Someone who buys products in a foreign country in order to sell them in his or her own country.

innovation A new idea or way of doing something.

investors People who put money into a company; their money grows if the company is financially successful.

latex A substance found in various plants that is used to make rubber and some plastics.

lay off To dismiss employees not because they are doing a poor job but because a company needs to save money.

line of credit An agreement to lend money, or supply credit, to an individual or company.

promote To encourage the use of a product among consumers by explaining its benefits.

quota A number or amount expected of an individual; if factory workers have a quota of 20 pairs of shoes per day, they are expected to produce that many by the end of the workday.

royalty A share of a product's proceeds paid to someone in exchange for an endorsement or other valuable contribution.

stock Shared ownership in a company by many people who buy shares, or portions, of stock, hoping that the company will make a profit and the stock value will increase.

traction The ability of an object to grip a surface; the texture of a shoe's sole, for example, can keep a runner from slipping.

trademark A symbol or name that belongs legally and exclusively to one company; it may also refer to something that is unique about a company.

INDEX

Adidas, 6, 17, 20, 24, 42

advertisements, 27, 37, 42

aerobics, 30

Air Jordans, 24

air pockets, 19

All Conditions Gear, 37

athletic apparel, 8–9, 20–21,
    30, 34, 37–41

basketball shoes, 13, 16, 19, 24

Blue Ribbon Sports, 5–12,
    13–19, 21, 42

Bowerman, Bill, 5, 6, 9–10, 12,
    16, 23, 42

Cortez, 10, 13, 17

endorsements, 23–27, 31, 42

golf, 37

headquarters, 36, 42

investors, 12, 21

Japan, 4–5, 13, 17

jogging, 9–10, 19

Johnson, Jeff, 6–9, 19

Jordan, Michael, 24, 25

"Just Do It," 27, 42

Knight, Philip, 4–9, 12, 13, 16,
    17, 19, 21, 23, 31, 33, 34, 41,
    42

latex, 16

layoffs, 31, 43

Marathon, 10

McEnroe, John, 24

Nike Town, 36, 37, 43

nylon, 10

Olympics, 10, 13, 24, 41, 42

Onitsuka, 4, 10, 13, 16–17

overseas factories, 33, 43

Prefontaine, Steve, 13, 23, 42

Reebok, 30

Rudy, Frank, 19

sales, 4, 5, 8, 10, 16, 19, 20–21,
    24, 30, 33–34, 36, 37, 42,
    43

soccer, 25, 34

stock, 21

Swift suits, 37–41

Swoosh, 13, 17, 42

Tailwind, 19–20

Tiger, 4–5, 8, 10, 13, 17

track-and-field, 4, 5–6, 13, 23, 27,
    41, 42

University of Oregon, 5, 6, 13, 42

waffle sole, 16, 42

women, 16, 25, 27, 37

Woods, Tiger, 27, 37

Books

Christopher, Matt. *On the Court With Michael Jordan*. New York: Little, Brown & Co., 1996.

Greenberg, Keith Elliot. *Bowerman & Knight: Building the Nike Empire*. Woodbridge, Conn.: Blackbirch Publishing, 1997.

Jordan, Tom. *Pre: The Story of America's Greatest Running Legend*. Emmaus, Penn.: Rodale Press, 1997.

Web Sites

Nike's official Web site
http://www.nike.com

Nike Town's online store
http://www.niketown.nike.com

Tiger Woods's official Web site
http://www.tigerwoods.com